FRED R(

RECOLLE

I was born in Varley Street, Miles Platting, Manchester, on 19th November 1884, and my earliest recollection is of when I was about four years old. My mother had a big mug of dough on the hearth in front of the fire, ready to bake bread, and it was rising nicely. My sister was about two years old and she was just beginning to toddle. I can see it now; she sat clean in this mug of dough! I also remember my father taking me on to Bradford Road to see a procession. In it was the Duke of Clarence, who was then engaged to Princess May, and he was coming to open a new wing in the Ancoats Hospital. He was in a landau pulled by two horses and there were a lot of horse soldiers in front. I remember my father lifting me up on to his shoulder so I could see. Very soon after that the Duke contracted scarlet fever and died. The Duke of York became engaged to Princess May and they became King George V and Queen Mary.

When I was five or six my father, who worked for the Lancashire & Yorkshire Railway Company, was transferred to the Blackburn district. So my parents, my sister and I went to live in Blackburn and I started to go to an infants' school there. The first thing I remember at that infants' school was standing on a form because I was the first to stitch a trouser button on to a piece of cloth. The button had four holes in it and the first child to stitch one on to his cloth was told to stand on the form. It was a big school and my sister and I used to run home across a big canal or river bridge. All the children who crossed it used to run for dear life, as Jack the Ripper lived underneath. Once, when we were running across the bridge, my sister's little red drawers dropped down. I picked them up, put them under my arm and carried on running home!

We lived with my grandma on Cemetery Road in Blackburn. It was a nice house, with a great big long garden in front of it. We had an uncle living with us. I think he was out of work and he must have been a bit of a betting man. When I came home from school for my dinner he'd send me for the midday paper, which carried the horse racing information. He used to say to me, "Go as quick as you can and see if you can get back before I count a hundred." It was quite a distance to the newspaper shop, but I used to try and race the trams, which were then drawn by great big steam engines, running my little heart out. When I got back to the doorstep with his paper, my uncle just started counting at 98 - I didn't realise that, I thought I had been clever and got home before he got to 100! I had no sense!

When my father first started work he was a furniture maker; he worked for a man called Spencer. Then he became a painter for the Lancashire & Yorkshire Railway Company - he used to paint the water chutes, those kind of things - and the bosses' houses, I

1

suppose! There were some railway companies in those days – the Lancashire & Yorkshire, the Manchester, Altrincham and South Junction Railway, the London & North Western, the Midland Railway, the Great Eastern, the Great Western, the Southern Railway... I was fascinated with railway engines when I was a boy. We used to go for our holidays to Fleetwood; my father got what were called privileged tickets for us. I'd go to the station at dinner time when the boats were coming in from the Isle of Man and see all the sickly folk – "Never again!" they used to say as they came off the boats! They would get off the boats, walk along the dock and go straight on to the station platform. I stood there for hours watching railway engines and people getting in and out of the trains.

My father once had the job of painting the Belfast Liners, which all belonged to the Lancashire & Yorkshire Railway Company. He took me right through one of them one morning. It was the "Duke of Clarence"; they all had names like "Duke of York", "Duke of Clarence" and "Duke of Lancaster". The Belfast Boats used to sail from Fleetwood. Sometimes, when he was at Fleetwood, which was every year nearly, a fisherman would sell my father a great big hamper of fish, which he brought home. We would supply all the neighbours with fish – every kind of fish you could imagine. But you had to get rid of them quickly in the warm weather!

When we stayed at Fleetwood for our holidays we used to have a bedroom, two shillings a night or something like that. Mother would take us down to the prom to sit on the sands, and every time we

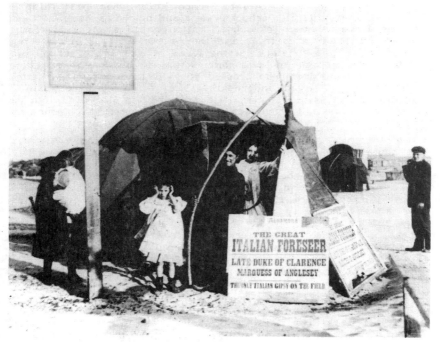

Gypsies on the sands at Fleetwood at the turn of the century

went we called at a toffee shop for twopennyworth of sugared almonds. Mother loved sugared almonds! She gave us one each, so of course she didn't have many left after the five of us had had one. We went back for dinner (Mother had to buy all the food and do the cooking) and then every night we used to go and listen to the pierrots on the beach. Some of them were very good, too.

I remember one dinner time when we were going back after being on the beach all morning; I let the others go on in front because I had seen some bananas – they had just been "invented" then! I saw them in a shop window and oh, I was dying for a banana! I'd got a penny in my pocket, somehow or other, I don't know how. When the others had got out of sight I bought this penny banana and I ate every bit of it quicksy!

When we were at Fleetwood we used to sail across on the little ferry boat to a place on the other side of the channel called Knott End, a very nice place. We used to spend an afternoon there.

The Lancashire & Yorkshire Railway Company's chief works was at Horwich, near Bolton, where they made the railway engines. No matter where he was working, in Lancashire or Yorkshire, my father had to report back every Friday night to Horwich. Sometimes it was ten or eleven o'clock before he got home. I remember one night it was late and Mother was upset; he hadn't arrived home and we found out later he'd been in a railway accident. His back was hurt so the railway company provided him with a belt, which he wore for the rest of his life. He died in 1938 when he was 78. He was a good man, my father.

I had all my illnesses when I was a little boy. I went to Southport Convalescent Home on two different occasions for three weeks at a time because I was so poorly, yet here I am at this age! I once suffered terribly with earache. I would lie on the sofa and my mother used to boil an onion and put the centre in my ear to try to help it. Then one Friday after tea my grandma, who lived opposite us, took me to a specialist in St John Street, off Deansgate. I went into the surgery and there was this older man, as I thought; Dr McEwan was his name. He put a reflector on his forehead and looked down my ear. After quite a time he took the reflector off, put it down and said to my grandmà, "Now take him home and give him a hot bath, as hot as possible, and put him to bed. In the morning take him to Mrs Dobson, 119 Oldham Road, Miles Platting." The next morning we went to Mrs Dobson's house. It was in the middle of a long row of terraced houses. My grandma knocked at the door and Mrs Dobson opened it and invited us in. She took us to the dining table in the kitchen. We sat down and then she brought out a stone jar full of leeches. She took out a leech and put it on my ear. I had to hold my head over the dish and by jingo, the blood that came out! Black and blue and red and all sorts of colours! Then, when the leech had had its fill it dropped off, dead, into the dish. There was no dressing, no mopping the blood up. I had to get my hankie out and hold it over my ear as we walked home. Mother had an awful night, changing pillow slips two or three times because they were saturated with blood. But I've never had an earache since that very moment, and I'm now 96! This doctor came to see me once and when I told him this story he started laughing. He said, "That never cured your earache!" I said, "What did? Because I've never had it since!"

On the day the Duke of York married Princess May in 1893 I went to a little celebration at our school, St Mark's. Mr John West, who was the founder of West's Gas Engine Works, gave the school a party. I always remember we were given a little paper bag containing an Eccles cake, a lemon bun and a little sandwich. When I was a little boy I used to pass a confectioner's shop and look in the window at the lemon buns. Oh, I did want a lemon bun! They were only a ha'penny each but I couldn't afford them. Then I got a lemon bun in this packet on this party day.

On another Royal occasion I went with a number of other boys and girls and climbed the hoardings, as we called them, by the side of the railway to see Queen Victoria in the Royal Coach. She was returning from opening the Ship Canal, or part of it. Fortunately for us, we sat near where the train entered Miles Platting Station, so it slowed down. We had a beautiful view of that old woman - but by God she looked a Sauerkraut!

I was named after my godfather, Fred Palmer, who owned a public house called the New Inn on Gibbon Street, near Ashton New Road. One day my mother sent me to my grandma Roberts, who lived near there and I got lost on Ashton New Road. I couldn't find my way home and every old man I saw with one of those round felt hats like parsons used to wear I thought was my grandfather and I went up to them. It was my godfather who eventually found me. He said, "What are you doing here, Fred?" I said, "I've got lost." So he took me home to Mother. He was one of the directors of Newton Heath Football Club, when they played in Bank Street, Clayton. In those days they used to let us boys in at half time for nothing. We use to go and stand round the ground and at half time they'd open the gates and we all went streaming in.

The shops used to be open all hours. We had a little shop on our road, Mrs Jones's, and she sold everything. We'd go to her for twopennyworth of bacon or a packet of sugar. We'd go to Marlon's bread shop for a tuppence ha'penny loaf. He'd put it on the scales and weigh it and if it was under he would put a make-weight with it, cut from another loaf. I often ate the make-weight on the way home - Mother just got the loaf! The milk cart used to come down the street and all the wives would come out with pint jugs to get their milk. I think it was three ha'pence a pint. They usually had a little gossip as the milkman served them from his churn. Every Monday afternoon an old man used to come round pushing a little dandy with a milk can on it containing buttermilk. He used to yell, "Buttermilk, a penny a quart!" By jingo, I've drunk some buttermilk! Every Tuesday Mr Tomlinson, a greengrocer who had his shop a long way from where we lived, used to come round shouting, "Isle of Man kippers, three ha'pence a pair!"

Our greengrocer, Mrs Jones, was known as "Donkey Jones". She was a little widow and had a cart with a donkey pulling it. She used to go to the market, as they all did in those days, at four and five o'clock in the morning to get loaded up. You'd see them all coming along Oldham Road. She had to go down Butler Street, half of which was very much higher than the other half, with a hill sloping down from the top. Her donkey cart was coming down one Saturday morning when the donkey decided to lie down on the slope. All the goods rolled off the cart and everybody helped her to pick them all up again and put them back. She was a good old

4

soul.

There were a lot of street singers in those days; people were poor, very poor indeed. It was common to see a man and his wife coming along the middle of the road and two or three children trailing behind, singing for the odd ha'penny. There used to be a lady singer who, it was reckoned, was a well-to-do person who was doing it for charity. She used to come round Bradford Road every Friday night singing, but nobody ever saw her face because she wore a mask all the time. She was a beautiful singer. There were organ grinders, mostly Italians from the community which I remember starting behind where the Daily Express works is now. (The ice cream carts started there too.) They used to come round with these little barrel organs held in front of them, with just a piece of wood hanging down to rest on. When they had finished playing they'd pull this leg up and go away. They always had a monkey with them, which used to sit on top of the barrel organ and then take a little tin cup round to collect the ha'pennies and run back again.

My mother and father went to St Philip's Church; we children went to St Mark's, just two or three hundred yards away from St Philip's. We went to St Mark's day school because when we went to live on Bradford Road we lived next door to a newspaper shop and their boy and girl went to St Mark's day school and so Mother sent us there. The newspaper shop was Crosdale's; he was a great Conservative. He used to deliver his own papers - no boys, of course, as boys used to sell papers in the streets on their own in those days. Men used to come in the horse and cart to the corner of the street and the lads would collect and pay for the newspapers and go on their rounds. It used to be a sight on Market Street in Manchester at four o'clock every afternoon to see all the ponies and carts starting off in one long procession and going to the stations with the newspapers. People used to stop and stare at them.

My father once made me what was called an alley board. This was a flat piece of wood with holes bored in it at intervals at one end. The holes were then numbered 1,2,3,4 and 5. You'd put the alley board on the ground and then a lad would kneel on the edging stone with his marble and roll it up and try to get it through one of the holes. If he got it through I had to give him the corresponding number of marbles. I was a marvel for winning marbles! Other children used to come and knock at our door for a ha'porth of marbles! I think I used to sell them 20 for a ha'penny. We used to decorate our tops with coloured paper so they'd look lovely when they were spinning round. The girls played skipping rope and bobbers and kibs and hopscotch. We all played cricket with a lamp post as a wicket, but when we saw the Bobby coming we'd all skip off round the corner to the entry until he'd gone.

We were frightened of the police because they always walked about with their truncheons hanging down by their side. They used to come down the entries in those days to see if your back doors were fastened. Once, when we lived in Blackburn and we were all in bed (I slept in a little back bedroom at the top of the stairs), I was woken by a light shining right into the back of the house. It was a policeman at the front door shining his light through the front door, which had been left open. My Auntie Emmie must have come home late that night and forgotten to close the door behind her.

St Mark's Boys' Brigade

One Christmas morning, when we lived in Miles Platting - there were five of us, three girls in one bedroom and we two boys in the back bedroom - we shouted to Mother to come and see what Father Christmas had left us. She said, "Come and see what he has left me!" We all went dashing along the landing into her front bedroom and there was a stocking hanging over the bed rail with a birch rod sticking out of the top. Mother was a strict woman! Once we had a ragbone man who used to come round and his mouth was a bit twisted, which affected the way he shouted "Ragbone!" We children were frightened to death of him! One morning Mother said, "I'll leave you lot to the bone feller" and she went across the road to her mother's house. We were frightened to death and screamed the house down! My grandmother said to her, "Oh, you are a hard madam! go back to your children!" My mother was very humorous, although she was not a strong girl at all.

Monday was washday. Every Monday morning I got up and made the fires, then I had to make the little boiler fire in the kitchen. Mother put all the washing into the boiler and afterwards pegged it on the line in the yard. It was a pretty long yard and there were entries between the rows of houses.

Once Father made a little fern case out of the living room window, a glass affair. There were plants and ferns and a little glass-topped aquarium in the middle with goldfish in it. I always remember once when the rest of the family had all gone to bed and left me studying in the kitchen. All at once I heard a tapping on the window. By jove! I closed my books and was upstairs like I don't know what! I was frightened to death! I told my mother and she couldn't understand what it was. But we found out a few days later, when we were all having dinner. The cat jumped up to sit on top of the case and, whilst it was scratching its ear, its paw was scratching the window at the same time!

My grandma was a midwife and all the children were born at home. Although we were only boys and girls, when we saw these women with great big lumps in front of them we knew what was going to happen! I've often seen a woman sitting on a chair on the front doorstep feeding a baby.

The little Jews used to come round mending windows. They had wooden frames on their backs containing pieces of glass of different shapes and sizes and they used to knock at your window: "Do you want a window putting in?" We lads used to shout after these Jews: "Who killed Christ?" A terrible thing to do. Then men used to come round mending doormats. They would sit on the flags, plaiting them and putting fresh pieces in. We always used to get a lot of people knocking on our door on a Monday afternoon. That was when they let the people in the workhouse have half a day out to go and see their relations. They used to come and ask for a slice of bread and butter or a cup of tea. My father's friend was one of the bosses in the Crumpsall Workhouse, Mr Bagshaw.

Jackie the lamplighter used to come round with his great big pole with just a little flicker of light at the top. He'd turn the tap on the lamp and light it every night and then he'd come round early each morning to turn them all out when the knockers-up were about. The knockers-up used to start at three o'clock in the morning, and generally they were women. We never had a knocker-

Piccadilly, Manchester, in the 1890s

up at our house and I've never had one. I've always woken at half past six every morning. Father used to leave the house at three o'clock if he was working on the other side of Yorkshire. We used to hear them: "Four o'clock!" they used to shout. "Nice morning!"

There were one-horse and two-horse trams in Manchester. I only fell off a tram once in all my life. I'd been on an errand for Mother to Oldham Street and I thought I'd be clever and get off near Varley Street before it stopped. I jumped off the wrong way, with my back to the horses, and went flat on my face! We only had trams on Oldham Road, Rochdale Road and Ashton New Road in those days. I remember we lived on Bradford Road when the first tram started down there. What a sight it was that night! The place was crowded as the illuminated tram came down the road.

I bet there was a fight outside every pub in Manchester on a Saturday night! We had a parson at St Philip's Church, Robert Catterall, a famous preacher. Every Saturday night that man put his coat and hat on and went out at eleven o'clock to go round the pubs and stop the fights that were taking place. It didn't matter whether it was a nice pub or a dirty place - there was always a fight outside! The men had got to arguing while they were having their drinks. That's how boys settled their differences in the day schools. It used to be common to see a crowd of lads, when school closed at half past four, going to the recreation ground to fight it out. Very, very common. I remember the Scuttlers - we called them Ikes - who wore red and blue stockings and scarves wrapped loosely around their necks.

There were nine or ten pubs on Bradford Road alone when I lived there. The gasworks was at the end of the road, just before you got into Philip's Park, and right opposite, at the end of the row was Hayhurst's pub. I went to school with two boys of their family and my cousin married the son. I remember John Hayhurst; he was in my class at school and he'd done something wrong at home. That lad was taken upstairs and tied to the bedpost and left there for three days. He didn't have a meal, only what his sister could take up to him unbeknownst to the father. There was a row of fifteen or sixteen houses and then another pub; right across the road was another pub - Cheadle's - I taught all their children. At the end of the row where we lived was another pub; I went to school with the son there. Across the road was another pub.

The girls at school had their hair down to their waists in plaits and the headmistress of the school next to the one I went to used to give a yearly prize to the girl who had the best dressed hair in the school. They had no nurses at school in those days. I've gone home and found creepie crawlies all over me and my coat many a time. We had these long desks in school and you had to walk behind and brush past the girls with their long hair. Every house had a small tooth comb on the mantelpiece, just for the girls' hair - and boys' as well, I suppose. Most of the houses were nice and clean, but some of them weren't.

We had an oil lamp in the middle of the table for lighting. We used to go to a shop in Gibbon Street, next door to my godfather's pub, on a Friday night with a can for tuppence worth of lamp oil. I remember I was just getting to the shop one Friday night when a woman came to me and said, "Where are you going, love?" I said,

"I'm going into the shop for tuppence worth of lamp oil." She said, "Just go across to that house for me. I'll mind your money while you come back." She took my tuppence and went off with it! I never saw it again!

Whit Week was the children's time in Manchester. It was a beautiful week for children. On Whit Sunday we used to walk round the parish – all the Sunday School scholars, parents, choirs, Bible classes and so on. Whit Monday was the morning for Protestants. We used to leave St Mark's School on Holland Street, not far from

The Queens Hotel, Miles Platting, at the turn of the century

10

Philips Park, at seven o'clock and we didn't get to Albert Square until nine. We used to walk all the way down Holland Street, down Woodward Street, past New Islington and down Union Street. There were about half a dozen cotton mills opposite the canal on Union Street. All the windows in these mills used to be crowded with girls looking down at the procession as we went along. As we walked through Manchester there were men selling "hokey pokey". They used to run along as we were walking, calling "Hokey pokey, two for a penny! Hokey pokey, two for a penny!" This was a slight piece of tissue paper containing ice cream.

We walked out of Albert Square according to the age of our church. The Cathedral boys and congregation walked out first, followed by the next oldest and so on. Often we were standing in that Square from nine o'clock until eleven, packed like sardines, as we were a new church. We used to walk out of the Square, right up Portland Street to Market Street, down Market Street to the Cathedral, round the Cathedral and up into Oldham Street, along Oldham Road to Varley Street, down Varley Street to the church and the day school. It would be two o'clock in the afternoon when we got back, absolutely weary! If it was a very hot day, the tar would be oozing out from between the setts on to the poor little girls' white shoes. They were full of tar when they got back. We were given a bun each at the school.

Bands always used to accompany the scholars. St Philip's, the next school to us, always had what was called the Tall Hat Band – Culcheth Military Band – as they always wore tall hats. There was Beswick Subscription Band, and we always had Ardwick Highland Band – they were dressed in kilts. We had that band for years and then one Whit Wednesday afternoon we went to one of the fields nearby or to Philips Park to have our buns and milk and play. The band began to play a dance tune and one of the fellows put his instrument down and got hold of one of the girls who was standing there and started to do a bit of a jig. The curate saw him and we never had that band again at St Mark's! We never had dancing at St Mark's. They had dancing at St Luke's just across the canal, but not at St Mark's. On Christmas Eve and New Year's Eve there were parties and we used to play musical chairs, find the slipper and so on, but no dancing! At ten to twelve we'd all walk out of school to the church for the service.

On Whit Thursday we had the scholars' trip. I've seen the time at St Mark's School when there were twenty-four lorries outside. We used to put the school forms on the lorry and fasten them so they wouldn't slip. We went to Flixton or Urmston, and we thought we were at the other end of Europe! One year we went to Greenfield, and it poured the whole morning in the farmyard where all the lorries were. So the teachers decided that was the end of it and we had to come home at dinner time. About half past four, when the Evening Chronicle teatime edition came out, I went past Crosdale's newspaper shop on the road where I lived. I can see the placard now outside that shop window. The Boer War was on and General Buller had relieved Ladysmith.

On my thirteenth birthday I was in Standard X7 at St Mark's school. I don't know how I got there, because you were supposed to leave school in Standard 7. But I got to X7 – I must have skipped a class. The headmaster was a terror – he always walked about with a stick cane in his hand - and on that day he came to the classroom door and I was sitting by myself, being in X7. Standard 7 was at the other end of the room. He said, "Now Fred, you're 13 today, you're a teacher." I had no idea! I didn't remember telling Mother what I wanted to be. "Go to Mrs Dunkley and help her with Standard 4." This I did and that's how I started teaching, at 2/1d a week. I had to wait until the end of the month for my wages, like the other teachers, and when I took my first 8/4d home to Mother she gave me a ha'penny back. I called at the toffee shop on the way to school and bought four aniseed balls, which would last me all day. The next year my wage doubled up to 16/8d, and the year after it was £1/13/4d and so on until I was 18.

One of my earliest recollections of when I was a pupil teacher was when I was still in short trousers - I didn't go into long trousers until I was fifteen. I wore short trousers and black stockings with garters round the top. I was teaching Standard 5 spelling, and I thought this lad wasn't spelling hard enough, so I rapped him on his leg with a ruler which I had in my hand. At half past four his father came for me; he must have been six feet tall and he chased me all round that school - I was terrified! The teachers ran after us, trying to stop him. I managed to get to a little classroom in the infants department and placed everything I could behind the door to stop him. To my horror, when I was going home that night, I found out that he lived next door to the school. I didn't dare pass that house for years!

When I was 13 I went to the pupil teachers' college in Aytoun Street, off Portland Street, for the half day; the other half I taught at school. One week it would be mornings at the college and afternoons at the school, and the next it would be mornings at school, afternoons at college. That went on for five years until I was eighteen - no wonder I was a good teacher, I had a good training!

I was a pupil teacher when Mafeking was relieved. I was at the pupil teacher's college in Aytoun Street and the teacher must have told us. We all jumped up, collected our books and went sailing down Aytoun Street into Market Street, which was one seething mass of people. I don't know how that crowd had got there in such a short time! There were people selling flags and whistles and hooters and all sorts of things. I will always remember that day.

Every Saturday morning for five years I walked from Miles Platting, near Philips Park (we lived quite near the entrance), to the Art School at All Saints. It used to be half past one when my friend Joe Jones and I got home for our dinners. He lived in Ridgway Street nearby. If it was the summer time when plums were about, men used to come around with them on handcarts - no boxes for them, all the plums were heaped up on the cart. They were called "egg plums", and we used to buy a pound for a ha'penny and eat them on Joe Jones' doorstep.

I went into long trousers when I was fifteen, and oh, I was embarrassed! I was at dayschool that morning, teaching. When I went to school and into the teachers' room, where all the teachers assembled before school started, they all looked at me. Miss Harper came up to me and said, "Who's spoilt Fred?" She was a dear soul, a lovely woman. She lived with her mother, who had a boot shop opposite St Paul's Church on Oldham Road.

We always went to Shudehill Market every Saturday night. All the young people did; there were no pictures or anything like that. Right opposite the Chronicle office there used to be the Hen Market, selling live hens, ducks and chickens in little boxes. I've seen men and women walking home along Market Street and Oxford Street on a Saturday night with their hens tucked under their arms. They would have to kill them themselves when they got home and cook them for dinner. All the stalls were covered over with tarpaulin and there were ice cream carts, cow heel stalls, black pudding stalls and trotters stalls. You'd see people standing there with their plates, eating away and enjoying themselves. Then we lads – there'd perhaps be half a dozen of us – would walk home along Oldham Road and down Butler Street into Holland Street. There was a chip shop in Holland Street called Mrs Beevers'. She was a widow with a lovely daughter who served in the shop, and I think we only went there to see the girl! We used to sit down at this long table and have our ha'porth of chips and then walk home, quite happy if that girl had served us.

The next morning the church bell used to ring at twenty past nine and then at half past nine the Sunday School doors were locked. If you were outside, you were late, and you got a late mark so that you had no chance of a first prize. We all had checks, little tin tokens with our names on them, which we had to give up to the Sunday School teacher when we entered the school and went into the

Shudehill Market in the 1890s

13

class. After Sunday School we were marched into church and those checks were not given back to us until we marched out of church. On the way to church one or two lads who didn't want to go sneaked out, but they were always found out in the afternoon because they had no checks to give in! One day I counted the tokens handed in - there were 964.

My father was standing at the door one day when he called in to me, "Fred, come here." There was a ragbone man going along the middle of the road with his handcart, shouting, "Ragbone!" My father said, "D'you see who that is? That's Billy Griffiths. He was a great full back for Newton Heath." There were no benefits and hundreds of pounds a week in those days. There was poor Billy Griffiths, selling ragbone.

The finest half-back line that ever existed in this world belonged to Newton Heath - Roberts, Duckworth and Bell, and when one of those was injured Alec Downey took his place. I remember the time when Meredith, Banister, Sandy Turnbull and Herbert Burgess all played for City and then got into the hands of a bookmaker. They were all sacked and they all went and signed for Newton Heath. Of course, Billy Meredith was the greatest outside right you ever saw in your life. He could pass the ball right on to Sandy Turnbull's head when he stood in the goalmouth. I remember once they were playing Aston Villa. Ashton New Road, Ashton Old Road and Bradford Road were crowded with people walking to the match (there were only horse trams then). It was said that Aston Villa were going to win by I don't know how many goals, but Newton Heath won 3-0. Jack Peddy, the centre forward, scored all three and I bet he didn't run two yards all the afternoon! He walked his way right round that Aston Villa team - he was a marvellous player!

Oldham Street at the turn of the century

Two brothers, Sandy and Alec Robertson, played for Newton Heath, and I always thought Sandy was a washout. Once, it was the last match of the season and Newton Heath were playing Woolwich Arsenal. If they lost they were out of the First Division. Late in the second half, Sandy Robertson received this ball somewhere about the full-back line and he dribbled the whole length of the field, right past the goalkeeper and scored the only goal of the match. That kept Newton Heath in the First Division.

The club had to move because an electricity works had been built next to the ground and you could hardly see the players on a Saturday because of the condensation from the cooling towers. Everybody was wet through – it was raining all the time. They let the people in nearby Stuart Street live rent free because the houses were so damp.

I always remember my father coming home for his tea once and saying, "I've heard the most beautiful sound today, Besses o'th' Barn Band." They were going on a tour – to Canada, I think – and before they left Victoria Station they played "All People that on Earth do Dwell". My father said it sounded beautiful in that Victoria Station.

The first time I went to the theatre I was sixteen years old. My father took me to the Theatre Royal on a Saturday afternoon to see the great actor Sir Henry Irving playing Shylock in "The Merchant of Venice". I remember queueing outside and there were buskers

Peter Street: the YMCA, Theatre Royal, Free Trade Hall and Comedy Theatre in the 1890s

15

singing and doing toss-tails-over and one thing and another. We sat in the gods, which cost threepence. As the first act opened, Irving appeared on stage after crossing a bridge in the scenery. He always used a walking stick when he acted in "The Merchant of Venice" and long before you could see him you could hear this stick on the Rialto Bridge as he was coming along. The crowd went absolutely wild, standing up and cheering! He was a fine actor. So was Ellen Terry, who was in the play with him. In those days I always thought Ellen Terry was his wife, which of course she wasn't. I saw Irving three times in one week. I went straight from day school to stand in the queue without any tea and paid my threepence to go in the gallery. I saw him in "Becket", which was a famous play, "Dante" and I saw him in a Russian play in which he goes mad - I forget the name. In 1905 he was playing in Liverpool and I picked up the paper one Saturday morning and on the top was "Sir Henry Irving Dies." He died in the theatre where he'd been acting in "Becket". In the play, Becket was killed on the altar steps of Canterbury Cathedral by the soldiers and the last words he said were, "Into thy hands, oh God." Those were supposed to be the last words Irving said in actual life. He had two sons, Laurence and H B Irving. Laurence Irving was a good actor.

On Good Friday everybody in Miles Platting used to go to Daisy Nook. This was a little village up in Failsworth; it still is, I believe. They always had a good do on Good Friday - wakes, little restaurants and a lake where you could have a row on the boats. I remember one particular Good Friday when moving pictures - the cinematograph - had just come out. I'd never been to one before, none of us had, and there was a show at Daisy Nook. It was called "The Bride's First Night". Of course, we were dying to see what this was all about! So we paid our pennies or twopences to go in and the picture came on, but we never saw the woman at all. There were two screens and she was supposed to be on the other side. Occasionally a blouse came over the top, and then her knickers, then a stocking, and that's all we saw of the Bride's First Night!

Much later on, I remember going to the pictures once in Clayton, and we heard the most marvellous singer I've ever heard, Laurence Tibbit. But I don't recollect the name of the picture.

When I was in my last year at pupil teachers' college, Joe Jones and I were on our way to Piccadilly and there was a girl coming in the opposite direction. She just glanced at us as she was passing and when she had gone I turned to Joe and said, "Wasn't she a lovely girl?" He said she was, and we saw her on several mornings afterwards. One morning we had got a bit further along than usual; we were at the approach to London Road Station when we saw her coming down the approach, so we knew that she came into Manchester by train. Well, I left the pupil teachers' college when I was eighteen, so I didn't see her again for some time. We had to pass a Queen's Scholarship exam when we had finished our pupil teaching - we became teachers then, Article 50s, as they were called.

Months after, the headmaster sent me across to St Mark's infants' school, which was across the road. As I walked down the passage and looked through the partition window, there was this girl in front of the class, teaching. By jingo, I lost no time! I became friends with her and we became engaged almost immediately. Our
16

engagement was different from these fancy engagements today. My mother said, "Bring Jessie to tea," so I took her one afternoon and after tea we walked to town. We walked down Oldham Street and I took her into a jeweller's shop and bought an engagement ring and put it in my pocket. We walked home from Oldham Street along Ancoats Lane, past where the Express offices are now, to Mill Street, where Ancoats Hospital is. Walking up Mill Street there is a bridge over the canal, and we leaned on this bridge, watching a boat being pulled along by a horse. I took the ring out of my pocket, took hold of Jessie's hand and put the ring on her finger -that's how we were engaged. No party, no anything. We were together for a long time; six years engagement and sixty-four years marriage. We went to Kays in Deansgate, which used to be behind where John Heywood's was, opposite the Daily Mail offices, and we had our photograph taken. I carried another one of her in my pocket all the time I was in the army, and I wrote to that girl every day that I was away.

I became a teacher in 1902, the year after Victoria died, and I remember Edward VII coming to the throne. He had peritonitis and was seriously ill and couldn't be crowned. Jessie and I walked down to the Cathedral because they were holding a special service to pray for his health.

A few years later I became a billiards fanatic. I became a really good billiards player and in 1907, 1908 and 1909 I won the first prize in the Billiards Christmas Handicap they held at the People's Institute where I attended. It was a lovely institute; I won a turkey each time. Of course, it was all feathered; we had to take the feathers out and clean it ourselves. Jessie and I got married in 1910, but I didn't give up billiards right away. I said, "I think I'll join the Christmas Handicap, Jessie." She said, "I hope you win a turkey again like you have been doing!" Of course, to her horror and mine, I didn't. I won a rabbit! Gradually I gave billiards up; I had taken up singing and that was going to be my hobby. I used to spend the evenings practising singing and going to concerts, but I always managed to have concerts where I could take Jessie. I never took her to a smoking concert because there was always a comedian who had very tasty jokes, and I wasn't going to have Jessie listening to those! I once went to a boxing match at Belle Vue and Jessie was disgusted with me. I didn't enjoy it very much!

One day I had been having my singing lesson and the singing master said to me, "You know, that uvula at the back of your throat is a bit too long and it makes you hoarse. I should have a piece of it cut off if I were you." So I went to see Doctor Dyas the next night. I can see him now, a great big six foot Irishman. He was a fine man. He used to drive about in a hansom or ride a bike and he would visit at all times of the day. I've been to that man at eleven o'clock on a Saturday night because I had a weakly mother. He used to say, "Come on. Get in my taxi and come to the surgery while I make up a bottle of medicine." (They had to mix their own medicines then, of course.) Well, I told him my singing master said my uvula was too long. Dr Dyas sat me on a chair - no fancy couches in those days! He brought out a pair of pincers, said, "Open your mouth," snapped a piece off and sent me home. No mouthwash, no anything! I was full of blood when I got home and I had a sore throat for a fortnight, but I was never hoarse after singing again!

The parson at St Mark's, Cannon Perry, was a very go-ahead man. He got in touch with all these money people and collected a lot of money. to have a country school built at Mobberley so that day school children could go and spend a fortnight's holiday. As it was his church, his day school children were the first to go. So I took forty boys for the fortnight. There were six teachers there; 240 boys in the school. We were a very happy band, they were a nice lot of fellows. On the first night we thought we'd get the boys to bed early so we could have a meeting to arrange a timetable; the school wasn't big enough to accommodate all 240 boys, so half of us would have to be outside if the weather was fine. We started this meeting and then there was a terrific row coming from the dormitories, which were across the path in the next field. When we got upstairs there wasn't one bed in position! They had been dragged about and pillows were flying all over the place. It was a terrible sight. Each two teachers had a bedroom at the side of the dormitory, with a window so that they could keep an eye on the boys. The fellow I was staying with said, "Have you got anything I can go round with to quieten them?" I gave him my razor strop and with the first blow he gave, he ripped it right down the centre! So I had no razor strop! However, we didn't have another minute's worry with those boys after that first night. As soon as tea was over we used to take them out for the longest walk possible. We took them such a long way one night – it was too far really. The poor lads were taking their coats and their waistcoats off long before they got back to school. Into bed they got and not a sound! We wore them out, but it was a good holiday – seven shillings for the week. I was married the same year.

The year before I was married I went to Sheffield to see United play Newcastle. It was the year they won the cup (1909). There were four of us, all teachers, and we got drenched. One of the others had an uncle in Sheffield and he invited us to tea after the match, so we had to buy new collars – ours were like tissue paper! We had a nice tea and then came home again. There were about thirty of us and we had booked a saloon – there was a barrel of beer put on board, not that I drank beer. Coming home the train stopped at Godley Station. Jessie lived at Hyde so I got out and walked to Hyde and spent the weekend there with Jessie and her mother. Jimmy Halse scored the only goal at Sheffield. I remember he came from a little football club somewhere in Surrey. Nobody had ever heard of him and I remember him playing his first match against Sheffield Wednesday at Clayton; they only won 1-0 and he scored the goal.

I used to play cricket with North East Manchester Cricket Club. We had two players in our team who signed for Lancashire, two stumpers. Lees Radcliffe was one; he lived quite near to us on Bradford Road. Archie MacLaren was the captain in those days, a real gentleman. Of course, there used to be six or seven gentlemen in the team – in those days they were not all professionals. There used to be the Gentlemen's gate and the Professionals' gate on to the field at Old Trafford. When the gentlemen were coming down the steps from the pavilion, one of the ground staff was there to open their gate and let them out. There was only one gentleman you never had to open the gate for – Walter Brearley, the fast bowler. He jumped over the top, always! He'd come down the steps and over the top of the gate he went.

Archie MacLaren was playing one day and **Lees** **Radcliffe** **was** stumping and ·he must have come out with **some** **swear** **word** and MacLaren heard him. MacLaren sent him off the field and he never played for Lancashire again!

I don't think I ever saw W G Grace. I saw McLaren many times, and Lord Hawk; C B Fry was a great cricketer; Gilbert Jessop – it was nothing for him to knock the ball out of the old Trafford ground into the roadway. He was a great hitter, played for Gloucestershire. I took Jessie to a match one Whit Monday; Lancashire were playing Yorkshire. Lancashire got bowled out twice in one day and Jimmy Hallows got hit on the head with a ball from Bowes and had to be carried off. Jessie was upset. "Oh," she said, "it's cruel. He ought to be put in prison!" Yorkshire beat Lancashire usually. Johnny Briggs was a great bowler, but the nicest bowler I ever saw was McDonald, who came from Australia. He had a beautiful run up to the wicket. Arthur Mold, who was quicker` than any bowler, used to take six strides to the wicket, that's all. Johnny Briggs was the great left arm spin bowler. I saw Larwood, he was a fast bowler, but the˙nicest bowler I ever saw in all my life was Brian Statham; beautiful action and a beautifully tempered lad. My friend taught him at Central High.

When I was scoring at the North East Manchester Cricket Club there were five balls to an over, and they were marked as the "5" on a dice. When there was a maiden over we joined the dots together to form the letter "M".

The Ardwick Empire

When I played for North East Manchester Cricket Club we had a
demon bowler called Charlie Baker. He only took five or six strides
to the wicket and never ran. We were playing Chorlton one day and
he got six wickets. He bowled six men out and hit the wickets each
time in one over; the fourth time he broke the middle stump! He
went on to sign on for Middleton. He got a very good job as a mill
manager at one of those big mills in Union Street. His mother and
father had a big tobacconist's and confectioner's business and he
married well. He wouldn't go to play for Lancashire, though they
wanted him. The cricket field we played on was bought by A V Roe
to build their factory next to Mather & Platt's. I remember seeing
my first aeroplane when I was at my father's for dinner one Monday – it was a sight to see, but we were frightened!

At the bottom of Peter Street, just before Deansgate, there was the
Tivoli Theatre, a right place that was! Three of us went one night,
and our wives said we could! There was a girl on there, singing
a song and scattering picture postcards of herself all over the
theatre. I had that postcard for a long time! Opposite the Tivoli
was the Albert Hall and coming along from there was the Gaiety.
Right opposite was the YMCA and next to that was the Theatre
Royal. Then there was the Princess Theatre, then the Palace
Theatre, then a bit higher up was the Ardwick Green Empire. There
were the Hippodrome and the Free Trade Hall as well. I heard all
the great singers at the Opera House.

I saw George Roby, and the best entertainer I ever saw was George
Formby – not the last one, his father. He always came to the Ardwick Empire and he always brought his beautiful wife, who stood
in the wings while he was singing. They talk about Harry Lauder,
but I don't think he was a patch on Neil Kenyon. He was a fine
Scottish comedian with a beautiful singing voice. I saw him many
a time. I saw Marie Lloyd, Florence Smithson; Zena Dare in Peter
Pan – she had a sister, Phyllis, and they were known as the Dare
Sisters.

I remember Sir James Fergusson; he'd been the Governor of Australia and he came and represented North East Manchester in Parliament. He used to come round before the elections with his tall hat
and white waistcoat, shaking everybody by the hand at every door.
Then the Labour people started; Johnny Clynes was the candidate.
I went to hear him speak at Holland Street School. I thought he
was an awful man! He had something wrong with his eyes. He
didn't wear spectacles, but they always seemed to be on the sore
side. He was a good speaker. Once James Fergusson went to a meeting in one of the schools nearby and said eighteen shillings a week
was enough for any working man. That did it! We never saw him
again – Clynes walked in! He became Home Secretary later on. He
was a good man.

I remember when Augustine Birrell was putting up for North East
Manchester. We were walking down Bradford Street, past a greengrocer's shop, and there were a few loose cabbage leaves lying on
the flags. He was just passing at the time in his landau and we
threw these cabbage leaves at him!

I went to the Free Trade Hall one night to hear Sir Edward Carson
when all this home rule business first started. The Free Trade Hall
20

was crammed and that man spoke for three hours without stopping and he never used a note. When he finished his speech everybody stood up and the hats went up to the ceiling. I also heard F E Smith, who became Lord Birkenhead later on. Winston was a great speaker, of course, but he always had that bit of an impediment with his tongue. Lord Balfour, Lord Roseberry, the Chamberlains were wonderful speakers.

I remember the Titanic going down - we thought it was unsinkable! Jessie and I went to a special Service at Manchester Cathedral. The captain's name was Smith, I think, and they were supposed to have sung the hymn, "Eternal Father Strong to Save," but I don't think they did.

I was in the army three years, but I made up my mind I wasn't going to learn anything! I was very disgruntled, although it wasn't that I was forced to go. When war broke out in 1914, practically the whole army was wiped out in the first twelve months. So Lord Derby came out with what was called the "Derby Scheme". They had Kitchener's picture in every pub window, with his finger out pointing, saying "Your Country Needs You." Everywhere you went, no matter how far past the pub, this finger was pointing at you! So a fellow teacher and I went down to enlist. Piccadilly, Portland Street and Mosley Street were worse than a football match coming out! I'd never seen so many young fellows on their way to the Town Hall, and when we got there, I'd never seen so many bare men in my life! You'd go into one room for one examination and then you'd walk, naked, to another room to have something else examined. I was passed A1 almost immediately and got the King's shilling, but the man I went with was rejected because he had flat feet - it was mostly infantry in those days and they didn't want flat feet in the infantry. Two or three days later a letter was sent to the school telling those of us who had joined up that we hadn't to go until we were released by the Education Committee, as teaching was a reserved occupation.

It was 1916 when I was called up, and Jessie was heartbroken, bless her dear soul. My father took me to the assembly point on the fish platform at Exchange Station. This was a long wooden platform where all the fish trains used to arrive from Fleetwood and Grimsby at three and four o'clock in the morning. I should think there were sixty or seventy men there , but I didn't know anybody. Later on, when we got talking, I found out that some had come from Cumberland, some from Yorkshire and some from Nottinghamshire. I was the only man from Manchester. I stood in the middle of this long line of fellows and the officer walked along, looking at us all. He inspected us again, then he came and stopped in front of me. He called me out and he said, "I want you to take these men to London." I was flabbergasted! Why the dickens had he chosen me? He gave me the railway voucher and I had to march these men up Market Street to London Road Station. I felt bitter that morning! I saw all the young fellows going off to work to the offices and here was I in the army, thirty-one years old, taking all these fellows to the station. I got them safely to London and then we marched off to Woolwich Barracks. When we were three or four hundred yards from the barracks, passing a pub, some of the fellows came out to me and said, "Do you mind if we just go to the lavatory at the back of this pub?" I said, "No, I'll wait for you."

A military inspection in Albert Square on the occasion of Lloyd George's visit to Manchester during the Great War

I could be waiting now – they never came back again! So my first job in the army was to report two absentees.

On that first day at Woolwich Arsenal we were taken to the canteen, a massive hut with three steps leading up to it. We had been issued our tin mugs and at the bottom of the steps was a pail of hot tea. We were given orders to take a mug of tea out of the pail as we mounted the steps to go into the canteen. We sat down at the dining table and someone gave us a thick slice of bread and butter each. Then another man came up with a pail of red cabbage, put his hand in it, took a chunk of red cabbage out and put it next to the bread on a plate in front of us. That was my first meal in the army! The only meals I ever enjoyed in the army were two Christmas dinners, because they were the only two days I knew the potatoes were peeled. Normally they were just dropped into the meat dish whole.

It was days before we got our uniforms; until then we were called "Civvies". "Fall in, the Civvies!" they used to call. Then we were sent to the tailor's department, who was supposed to measure us. He never saw the clothes I got! I had to spend I don't know how much getting them cut short – I was going to look decent if I was nothing else!

I was trained at Park Royal and I'd been there about six or seven weeks when a group of us were called out (they'd already picked the chaps to go to France). The sergeant walked behind us. "Haircut!" he said to one fellow, then the next, "Haircut!" I was picked out and so I went to the barber's and had a haircut. My hair didn't need cutting, but by jingo he cut it! We paraded at two o'clock and the sergeant came round again. "Haircut!" he said – to me again! I went to the barber's and he said, "What do you bloody well want?" "I want my hair cutting." "There's nothing to cut off!" "Well, the sergeant has sent me back to have my hair cut!"

Interestingly enough, I returned to Park Royal in 1925. I was with five other teachers who were detailed to take a hundred children to the state exhibition at Wembley by train. The place they took us to sleep for the night was the very camp where I had slept as a soldier.

After Park Royal, about fifty of us were sent to Devonport. We paraded in this great big barrack yard – there were lots of barracks in Devonport – naval barracks, air sea barracks and so on. We all assembled in a line and the regimental sergeant major – he looked a horrible man to me, a big, tall fellow – came up and inspected us. Then he went and stood in front of the line and shouted out, "Are there any clerks here?" I looked down the line. I didn't see any hands showing so I put mine out. "Come with me," he said. We were just mounting the steps into the offices when I said, "I'm afraid I've told a lie. I'm not a clerk, I'm a school teacher." "Oh," he said. "Just the man we want." So they gave me a posh job in the office. I was clerk to the Captain of Transport for the South Western Command all the time I was at Devonport.

I had not been in the army long when my mother died. They sent me home right away on leave, no trouble at all. At the end of my leave the parson whose church I attended said, "You want another day or two off." So he sent a telegram to Devonport and they

MILES PLATTING, based on the 1922 Ordnance Survey. 1 Varley Street,
Queen Victoria. 3 St Luke's School, where he was headmaster for 20
School. 5 Morgan & Crossley's works. 6 Hardman & Holden's works. 7
at the age of 13 in 1897. 9 Holland Street School. 10 St Philip's, Fred R

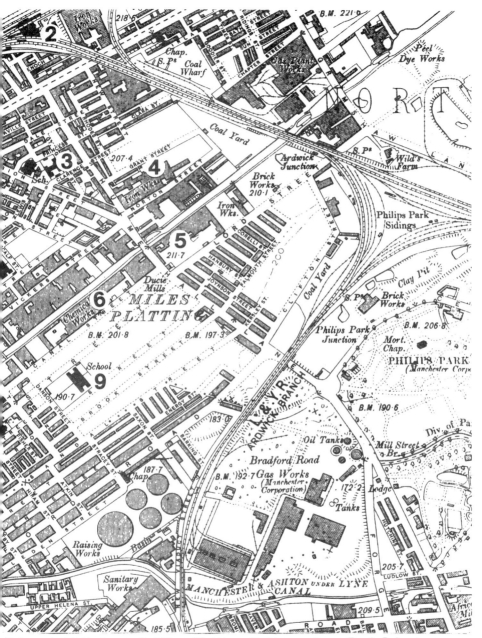

Roberts' birthplace. 2 Miles Platting Station, where Fred Roberts saw
. 4 West's Gas Engine Works; Mr West was a benefactor of St Mark's
d's Mill. 8 St Marks School, where Fred Roberts became a pupil teacher
s' parents' church.

allowed me another two or three days' leave. I only had one other leave besides that the whole three years I was in the army. I only saw my wife twice all the time I was there. Oh I was miserable! I wrote a letter every day to Jessie. On the second night at Devonport I walked across the barrack yard to the canteen and when I opened the door I saw a piano. I walked back to my bed, took out my writing tablet and wrote another letter to Jessie. I said, "Please send me some songs." A day or two afterwards a whole packet arrived. From then on I used to go to the canteen night after night, playing the piano and singing these songs. Then the news spread! Officers came from the naval barracks and asked if they could have me for the night to sing at a do they were having. So I passed my time singing - I did thank God he'd given me a voice!

I didn't go overseas, my singing saved me. On two occasions an officer came with a list of people who were being sent to France, and my name had been crossed out because I had an engagement that night at an officers' mess. I was lucky.

My job at Devonport was in transport administration. When somebody wanted a lorry to move something from one camp to another, or an ambulance, or a car for an officer, I organised it. Once, a girl telephoned and said she wanted a car for so-and-so; I didn't hear who it was for. I said, "Well, you can't have one, there are none in." She banged down the telephone and almost immediately the bell rang and my captain wanted to see me across the barrack square. He said, "You've done it! You've refused a general a motor car!" I said, "Well, I didn't know!" and the captain said, "He's threatened to send you to France anyway!" I didn't go to France, thank God.

Captain Crale was a fine man; he'd been to war and was wounded. He always had a cigarette holder, smoking a cigarette. I used to go to Plymouth in the middle of the night and then telephone the captain to tell him when a hospital ship had arrived. I went down to Plymouth Station once or twice, and oh, if you'd seen the sights I saw on that station! Some of the nurses were magnificent, they way they dealt with those terribly injured fellows without arms and legs. Once I sang before some wounded soldiers in one of Aggie Weston's hostels. I was so sorry for them. I met a tenor there who lived in Liverpool - Bert Elam - he sang a song, then I sang one, then he said, "I wish we had a duet." I had one among the songs Jessie had sent me - "Battle Eve", just the right thing. We sang it and they did enjoy it.

I went to church in Devonport, sitting on the back pew. One time I was singing away when I saw a sailor three or four pews in front of me. I thought, "That looks like George Robinson." I'd been to his wedding and sung for them; his family were friends of my mother. Then he turned round, as he'd recognised my voice. We met several nights after that. Then he came one night and said, "I won't see you again for a bit, the ship's been repaired and we're sailing tomorrow." His ship was torpedoed the very next morning and he drowned. His wife was very upset; they were expecting a baby. After the war she used to come round to our house and ask me how he had looked; he was a nice boy.

My brother was called up and only three days later he was in the trenches in France. He never had the slightest bit of training; they

26

were so hard up for men. Of course, he died; he got a chest complaint and died later on.

I used to play cricket with Jack Entwistle; his father kept the Brown Cow on Butler Street. Jack was courting a lovely girl, Emmeline Wallace - her father had a pub too - and when the war came Jack joined up and trained as an officer. I don't know why they did it, but many a young man would come home on his first leave and go off and get married. A lot of those girls never saw their young men again. Jack Entwistle married Emmeline and then he was sent to Italy. He was killed on the very first day he walked on to the battlefield. Emmeline never married again, and she lived to a ripe old age. It just broke her heart. It was a terrible war.

After about twelve months at Devonport I was transferred to Winchester and put in the artillery. So I had to work on guns there, something I liked very much, I'll tell you! I had one on my foot that nearly killed me! I used to go down to Winchester Cathedral every Sunday night I had free with another soldier, and one night as I was coming out I was touched on the shoulder by one of the officers of the church. He said, "The next time you come to church, will you come and sit in the choir stalls?" So from then on I went and sat in the choir stalls at Winchester Cathedral. The nights I wasn't going to church I used to go and sit with the other fellows in the barracks. There were some right types in that army! Several times I was on night duty with an officer and he would tell me to meet him at twelve o'clock at such-a-place. He was a fine lad. We were walking round one night when we saw a light in a hut about fifty yards away. I knew what they were doing; they were playing cards! The officer didn't say, "Will you go and catch those fellows?" He said, "Go up to that hut and turn the lights out." I opened the door and turned the lights off and there was such a scampering of those fellows away from the table where they were playing - the table was knocked over!

Once I was on sentry duty with another fellow at a sports contest. The sports field had to be guarded because there was a lot of equipment in it. Two of us would walk round one half of this huge field and another two sentries patrolled the other half. We walked round and came to a farm gate. It was a lovely evening and as we stood at the gate, looking up the road, two girls came along on the other side. When they got almost opposite to where we were standing, they came across the road to us and started talking. We hadn't been talking many minutes when the officer walked up. We were both booked and had to appear before the General the next morning. The following day he gave me such a lecture: "Have nothing to do with girls, they're a danger to everybody!" Much to my delight, I didn't take his advice!

The fellows in the army were a rough and ready lot, but they seemed to be kinder to the ones who had already been to the war. They had need to be, because these men had gone through a lot. You used to get a late pass which allowed you to come back to barracks at one o'clock in the morning; but they used to come in at three or four o'clock. How they got into that camp I don't know, because it was surrounded with barbed wire.

One night a fellow walked in, and he did look upset and sad. He

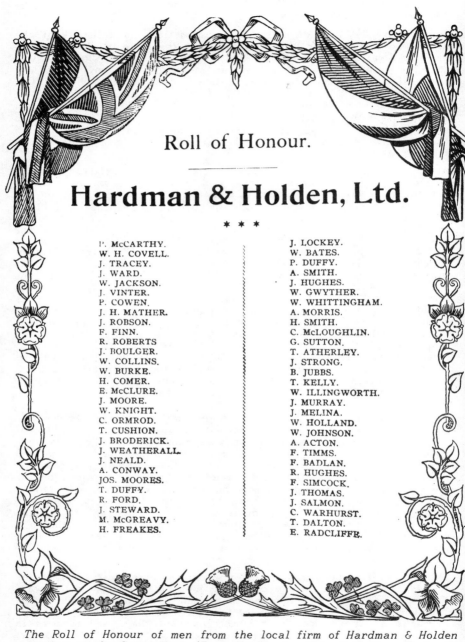

Roll of Honour.

Hardman & Holden, Ltd.

* * *

P. McCARTHY.
W. H. COVELL.
J. TRACEY.
J. WARD.
W. JACKSON.
J. VINTER.
P. COWEN.
J. H. MATHER.
J. ROBSON.
F. FINN.
R. ROBERTS
J. BOULGER.
W. COLLINS.
W. BURKE.
H. COMER.
E. McCLURE.
J. MOORE.
W. KNIGHT.
C. ORMROD.
T. CUSHION.
J. BRODERICK.
J. WEATHERALL.
J. NEALD.
A. CONWAY.
JOS. MOORES.
T. DUFFY.
R. FORD.
J. STEWARD.
M. McGREAVY.
H. FREAKES.

J. LOCKEY.
W. BATES.
P. DUFFY.
A. SMITH.
J. HUGHES.
W. GWYTHER.
W. WHITTINGHAM.
A. MORRIS.
H. SMITH.
C. McLOUGHLIN.
G. SUTTON.
T. ATHERLEY.
J. STRONG.
B. JUBBS.
T. KELLY.
W. ILLINGWORTH.
J. MURRAY.
J. MELINA.
W. HOLLAND.
W. JOHNSON.
A. ACTON.
F. TIMMS.
F. BADLAN.
R. HUGHES.
F. SIMCOCK.
J. THOMAS.
J. SALMON.
C. WARHURST.
T. DALTON.
E. RADCLIFFE.

The Roll of Honour of men from the local firm of Hardman & Holden serving in the Great War. (From Manchester City Battalions Book of Honour, published in 1916)

was a very tall young fellow, carrying his kitbag. There was one empty bed and he walked up to it. He just nodded to us as he went past. He sat down on the bed and started to take his tunic off and got undressed and then he put his pyjamas on - that was a thing we hadn't seen in the army! When he put them on he knelt by the bedside and said his prayers. There were half a dozen fellows playing cards, swearing and carrying on in that room, but it was absolutely dead silent when that man dropped on to his knees. Not a word was spoken. They stopped playing cards and I can see those heads now, all turned round, looking at him. Then the young man got up, got into bed and that was the end of that. I thought, "By jingo, you're a brave fellow." I wouldn't have said my prayers like that - I said mine under the sheets!

I was demobbed when I was at Winchester - they got me up at five o'clock one morning to get me ready. I had to go to London first by train and then from London right across to Whitchurch, where all the soldiers were demobbed in those days. When I got there they took my razor from me, my brush, comb and my little enamel mug, which was the first thing they gave me when I joined the army. That mug was used for everything - some fellows used it for their shaving water as well as for their cups of tea and coffee. They took my greatcoat off me, they took my puttees off me (I don't know why they took those!) and they took one shirt (they supplied me with two when I joined). I came home with my khaki trousers, my khaki coat, a shirt and my shoes. I arrived home on a Friday afternoon and knocked at the door in Barrington Street and there was nobody in. Jessie had gone shopping with her mother. However, I had a friend on North Road and I stayed there until she came back. I was supposed to have a month's holiday and I was paid £6-10-0 demobilisation gratuity for the month.

I came home from Whitchurch on the Friday and on the Monday I said to Jessie, "I'm going to school. I can't have a month off." When I turned up at St Mark's the headmaster was very glad to see me as they were two or three short - some teachers hadn't been demobbed yet. On the Tuesday morning the Manchester Education Committee's Inspector turned up and I was sent for to the head-master's desk. We were terrified of that Inspector - 3,000 teachers in Manchester were terrified of him! He sat at the headmaster's desk and I stood there. "What are you doing here?" he asked. "I've come home to teach." "How do you know I wanted you?" "Well," I said, "I hoped you did." "Well you never know. Besides, you've no business coming home!" He gave me such a lecture, but at length he said, "All right, we'll let you off this time. Go back to your class." So that's how I was demobbed!

When I first started teaching all the "council" schools were called Board Schools, and the officers who hawked you back to school when you had been away were called Board Officers. In Mill Street, next door to Ancoats Hospital, was a home for truants. I remember the Chief Board Officer, a little fellow with a bent leg - how he managed the job, I don't know - who used to come to school if there had been somebody reported for being truant for a day or two. He would come into school and ask Mr Turner, our headmaster, if a certain boy had come to school. If the boy was present, the board officer would ask his teacher if he could go to him. Then the board officer would get hold of the lad by the coat neck, lift him out of the desk and hawk him off to Mill Street. They kept them there for a day or two and made them clean floors, steps and stairs and so on.

We had an Industrial School at Ardwick. The truants' schools were just ordinary schools where the truants went for punishment; they went home at night.

There was a lot of work on the canals then. There was Holland's cotton mill, Hardman & Holden's chemical works, Morgan & Cross-

---

EDUCATION COMMITTEE.

Mr F Roberts is a student who compels the admiration of all who know him. He is most deservedly popular with his fellow-students and the staff. He is a man of sterling personal qualities and is perhaps the finest teacher in the college.

He is exceptionally gifted as a singer and has an excellent record as a student of music.

He is public spirited to a high degree and has rendered fine service to the college on the social side.

During his period of school-practice he gained the highest commendation.

His manner and methods are alike excellent.

He handles his class with the utmost skill and sympathy. He has an infinite fund of patience.

He takes the greatest pains in the preparation of his lessons and especially in the provision on suitable and telling illustrations.

Mr Roberts is moreover a man of the highest integrity and will exercise an inestimable influence for good amongst his pupils.

He will greatly strengthen any school staff.

Albert Mercer.
(Normal Master)

A copy of the testimonial from the Manchester Education Committee after Fred Roberts' two years at college, c1921

ley's brake lining works, plenty of them. When the canal boats came to unload, which would take a day and a night or longer than that, the boat familes used to send their children to school; they were called boat children. They had their own little registers and they used to come to our school; nice children. The wakes children did the same. There used to be a wakes at Albert Memorial Croft on Queens Road, just before Cheetham Hill Road. There was a family there called Bostock and every year their three children, while they were of school age, came to St Mark's school. I don't know why they picked St Mark's, because they'd pass other schools. You could tell they were brothers and sister; beautiful complexions and as clean as new pins. Only a few years ago, just before Jessie died, a man, a gypsy he called himself, used to give a little half hour talk every week. He was called Bostock - I bet he was one of those lads.

We also had half-timers at school. When a boy or girl got to Standard 5 - 11 years old - they could go on working half time if they wanted to. They all went to the mill at six o'clock in the morning, poor little things. Of course, in the afternoon they were half asleep. You didn't want to wake them, you knew they were tired.

A bargeman had a hard life. That man had to go to the stables first thing in the morning, get his horse out of its stable, feed and harness it and walk it to wherever the barge was tied up. During the day he had to open and close all the lock gates as he went along, cross the bridges and then take the horse back to the stables at night, feed it, groom it and then bed it down - all for fourteen shillings a week.

After teaching at St Mark's for some time, I went to college for two years - that was an experience. I got a lovely testimonial from the principal of the college, in which he said that, "Mr Roberts is probably the finest teacher in the college." There were 150 men there, all principal teachers. When I came out of college I started teaching at a very posh school in Newton Heath - Brookdale Park School. I had been teaching there some time when an Inspector walked into my room to tell me he had a vacancy at Holland Street Secondary School, Miles Platting. It was a big school in those days - 700 children (1922). He said, "Now we inspectors and the Director, Mr Spurley Hey, all know how fond you are of Miles Platting and how well you get on with the people there. Would you like to go and teach there?" I told him I was very happy where I was at Brookdale. He said, "Yes, and the headmaster's very, very pleased with you. But would you like to go?" Of course, I couldn't refuse, so I went. I had the happiest six years of my teaching life at Holland Street Secondary School, and it was from there I became a headmaster. Although I had only been there six years they gave me a leaving present of a typewriter, which came in very useful when I became a headmaster.

I was appointed headmaster of St Luke's in October 1927, but I hadn't to start until the 4th January 1928. New Year's Day was a Friday and we started the following Monday. When I got my first month's pay, they'd taken the salary off for January 1st, 2nd and 3rd, although I was still working for the same education committee! On my way down to the school on that Monday morning I was the most miserable man in the town! I had to walk through Philips

Holland Street School

Park, which was a lovely park, and I thought, "I wish I'd never applied for this job. I don't want to go." I knew that three of the fellows on the staff had applied for the job themselves, so it was a bit awkward, really. I didn't know them, so I had no idea what they were like. I had seen the previous headmaster once - he'd been there all his life and I think he was the first headmaster there. However, when I got near to school I braced myself and said, "Oh well, I've been made the headmaster and the headmaster I'm going to be." I walked into school and I saw four or five fellows and two or three women huddled together talking, so I went up to them and introduced myself. They all said, "Good morning," and I went to my desk, opened it and got the registers out. Then I rang the bell at ten to nine. Well, I'd been warned about that by the Inspector, who'd been to see me several times about the school. The last headmaster was an old man and he'd let the school go. The Inspectors had gone to look at the school and found the children out playing at a quarter past nine and twenty past nine. So at ten to nine I rang the bell for the children to be brought in. I went to the yard door and saw all these lines of boys (I didn't have the girls for the first two or three years) - Standard 1 up to Standard 7 - and the teacher said, "Turn", to walk into school. I said, "Just a minute. I want to have a look at them." So I walked round all these lads and looked at their hands and their faces and their shoes and clothes. When I got to the top class there was a boy, John Harris, as tall as I was nearly, and he hadn't been washed for months. I said, "Go home and get washed. Get your clothes brushed and get your shoes cleaned." The boy never came back. I thought, "This is a fine way to start a headmastership, a lad not coming back." But his mother came to school at dinner time. She said, "What have you sent our John home for?" I said, "Why, did you see he was John when he got home?" "Yes." "Did you see anything wrong with him?" "No." "Well, I did!" "Mr Shufflebottom never sent him home." "It's not Mr Shufflebottom's school. It's Mr Roberts' school now, and as long as I'm here, he'll have to do what I say!" And by jingo, I'm sure that news spread around Miles Platting! In fact, about four or five years ago I went to open a bazaar at the school and one of my old scholars, who's now 62, was asked to move a vote of thanks to me. When he got on to the platform, the first thing he did was look down at his shoes to see if they were clean. Well, the crowd roared! And they all started singing, "For he's a jolly good fellow." He said to me, "Do you know, Mr Roberts, if I'd been in church and I'd seen you coming towards me, I'd have had to look at my shoes to see if they were clean!"

I had only two spots of trouble with parents in that school, and I was there twenty years. I had only been there a few weeks when the teachers came to me and said, "Whatever you do, don't get across White." I said, "Who's White?" They said, "A great big fellow who lives at the second house across the road. He sits in his bedroom all the day and if there's a class out doing PT and the teacher happens to push a child, he shouts, 'Better not do that to my child! I'll be after you if you do!" He knocked the attendance officer off his bicycle and threatened to kill the last headmaster!" I said, "Well, I won't get up against him if I can avoid it." But unfortunately one of his boys was coming to school then. Two of his children had left, but he had five at the school and the eldest boy was in Standard 7. He was just as big as his father, and he

Classroom at Holland Street School

hadn't a grain of sense. He came late every morning, so after a few days I said to him, "I'm getting tired of you coming late. What do you come late for?" He said, "I've got to take my sister to the infants' school." Well, the infants' building was part of the school. You've only to cross the road. I told him, "If you come late tomorrow, I'll punish you." Of course, he didn't come the next morning. That morning I was taking the whole school, because the teachers had got far behind with their book work, and I thought I'd give them three-quarters of an hour to pull themselves up. While I was taking the boys, a knock came to the classroom door and I thought to myself, "This is White." I opened the door and there was this great big fellow standing there: "What's this? Threatening my lad?" I said, "I don't know who I am talking to." "You're talking to White from across the road. What's this, threatening my lad?" I was frightened to death of him! I said, "If you're going to talk to me like that, Mr White, you must step inside." I thought, "I'll have the lads to help me, if nobody else!" "I'm not coming inside." "Mr White, if you're going to talk to me in that threatening manner, you're going to step inside of this classroom and I'll talk to you then." "I'm not coming inside." "Well then, stop out." I closed the door in his face. It was a great big wooden door and I expécted him to start kicking at it. But there wasn't a sound. You could've heard a pin drop! So I went back to the children. All the lads' heads turned back again –they had all been looking at the door, hoping I'd get a good hiding, perhaps! At about a quarter to twelve I was sitting at my desk when a knock came to the door near my desk. It was a woman. I said, "Good morning." She said, "I'm Mrs White from across the road." I said, "Oh are you? Good morning, Mrs White." "You have insulted my husband." "Why?" "Closing the door in his face like you did. He's never going to speak to you again as long as he lives." And that man never did. I said, "Well, he should have behaved himself. He came in such a threatening and nasty manner that I had to close the door in his face."

Many's the time since he's been standing at his door when I've been past and we've never looked at each other. After a year or so he was taken to Baguley Hospital. He became very ill and he wrote me a lovely letter, thanking me for what I'd done for his children at school and telling me that his two eldest, the working ones, were giving a bit of trouble to their mother and would I go across and have a word with them. Of course, I didn't. I wasn't going to enter anybody's house.

The other spot of trouble occurred after a medical inspection. I'd had the nurses and doctors in all morning and a nurse came to my desk in the afternoon with the names of about eight children, and they were all in Standard 5, Mr Parker's class. I walked up to Mr Parker's class and who should be standing there by his desk but Michael Wells. He had been a little pest all morning, and I asked, "What's he doing out here?" Mr Parker told me what he had been doing so I took out this strap which I always had in my pocket and gave him a stoke of it. Then he carried on alarmingly, nearly bringing the school down! Yelling and crying – he'd never done that before. When I looked, there was his name on the nurse's list. I thought, "Hello, you know your father or your mother is coming, so you're going to create a bit of a commotion." I got the lads the nurse wanted into a line, walked them through the class-

St Luke's Class I, 1925

rooms, opened the door leading to the staircase and there was Wells' father. "What's to do, Mike?" "Mr Roberts punished me." "I'll take you away from this school." I said, "You jolly well won't! He's my property until four o'clock. His name is marked on my register so he's my property. He's yours after four o'clock and by jingo, if he was mine I'd know what to do with him when I got him home!" But Mr Wells carried on and carried on and then he leant down to Mike and said, "What did he punish you with, Mike?" I said, "See, I punished him with this, and if you don't believe me I'll give you a bit of it too!" He went as quiet as a mouse and didn't utter another sound. Then he went upstairs to the doctor and fairly got dressed down. The doctor said, "I've known Mr Roberts for a very long time and if he's punished your lad he jolly well deserved it and don't you ever dare come to this school again complaining." That boy, when he was twenty or twenty-one, joined the navy and I got a lovely letter from his father, from the very same man, thanking me for what we had done at school.

Parents used to come to me and say, "Will you speak to our Alice?" "Will you speak to our Henry?" When I asked why, they would say, "Ooh they have been giving a lot of trouble at home. But we've only to mention your name and all goes quiet!" I thought, "Well, that's nice!"

I remember when Neville Chamberlain went across to Germany to have a talk with Hitler, and word came through that peace had been signed between them. It was in the newspapers in the afternoon. I was going home from school when I heard somebody shouting, "Fred!" I looked and there was a girl with her head out of a car door. It was Doris Ridley, whom I'd known since she was seventeen. "Isn't it splendid news?" she said. She was with her father, a Wesleyan preacher. I said, "What?" "The peace!" "Yes, I hope it is." Of course it wasn't. He was an old diddler, Hitler was. The next year my father was ill, and he didn't want war. He died soon after, so he didn't have any war.

I've only been out of this country once in my life, when Jessie and I went to France for three weeks, and I didn't enjoy it really. It came about because two friends (he was a French master at Central High) had arranged a holiday in the South of France with their uncle and aunt. At the last moment the uncle and aunt dropped out, so they asked us to come. We went on the Friday we closed school, taking the car right from our door to the coast. We stayed on the coast for the weekend and on the Monday morning we sailed across to France. I was frightened to death! I'm absolutely terrified of the sea - I always have been - I clung to the mast the whole way across the English Channel! We used the car to travel through France to the Mediterranean, where we had booked a hotel - 9/6d a day each for ten days. It was a beautiful hotel, with its own private beach. We went to Cannes and Monte Carlo and all over the place, then we came back again the same way. We got home on the Tuesday of the last week of the holidays and on the Wednesday morning, late in August, I received a telegram from the Director of Education, telling me to open the school on Sunday to register the names of children whose parents wanted them to go on the Evacuation. So I got in touch with the caretaker and had the school opened, like all the other schools in Manchester.

St Luke's was open all that Sunday and the parents came with

Oldham Road before the redevelopment. On the left is the White Hart Hotel and Collyhurst Street. The opening of Varley Street is hidden on the right

their children. I had one or two nasty dos with parents because they demanded to know where the children were going and I couldn't tell them. The teachers didn't know, the scholars didn't know and I had been sworn to secrecy by the Director. They were evacuated the next Friday, September 1st. The war broke out on the Sunday morning, the 3rd. That Friday was a beautiful day and all these children (250) were gathered in the playground with their parents. I was just heartbroken to think I was taking those children away from their parents. The children didn't know where they were going; the parents didn't know where they were going. I had a prayer in that yard with the parents and the children before we set off.

When we got to London Road Station approach it was one seething mass of children. I wondered what would happen if Hitler came and dropped a bomb then. All the children were going away on the very same day from all over Manchester. I believe Exchange and Victoria were the same, just seething masses. We got on to the train and I knew we were all going to Bramhall, which I disagreed with, as I thought it was not far enough away. I got on very well with the Bramhall people, although several weren't very nice. One lady in particular, an actress, had two of my children, and they had to have all their meals in the garage. But most of them were well treated. I particularly remember the Brown family – Affleck and Brown had a big shop in Oldham Street. One of the Browns lived in Bramhall and he had one of my girls, Ann Hall. She was a poor

Some Salford children during the Evacuation

girl and had the time of her life with the Browns. She came from a poor home, but was nicely dressed, very clean and very clever. The Browns didn't want to part with her when the following Easter came round and the children had to go home and back to school. That girl spent every holiday during her teenage years with that family at Bramhall and when she was married they had the wedding from their house. Mr Brown also found her a good job in the General Post Office. There are some happy memories connected with the Evacuation.

Then came the big Blitz. That was a terrible night – the Town Hall was blitzed and I don't know where wasn't blitzed. The next morning I found pieces of shrapnel all along our path and I said to Jessie, "Well, I'm going to see if the school is still standing." So I walked all the way from our home in Ashton on Mersey to St Luke's and found the school was still standing, much to my relief. Then I decided to go and see my sisters. I had three sisters, who lived together; we had a sickly mother and they had sacrificed marriage to look after her. I went to Bradford Road and found half of their house was down. They'd had a bomb on top of it. Fortunately, they'd been lying on a couch under the stairs, and that had saved them. All the windows were gone, the doors were gone, the bedroom doors were off, but the strange thing was that there was a plant in the window and not the least bit of harm had come to it. The flowers and the leaves were still on it, yet the windows had all gone out! Four people in the house behind were killed outright by a land mine. I can understand the bombing round there because it was near Bradford Road gasworks and quite near to the Park Station and Miles Platting Station. There was plenty of industry around, like Mather & Platt's, Dempster's the boilermakers' and West's gas engine place.

St Luke's school closed in 1981 because the numbers had dwindled and the remaining children were sent to another school. I was invited to the farewell do. The headmaster and the school secretary kept phoning me, saying, "Oh do come, you'd be surprised at the number of letters we've had and they've all said, 'Will Mr Roberts be there?'" (I never had a school secretary. I had to do everything myself; registers, bank, dinner tickets, savings certificates, everything.) Well, I went to the do and there were people there who had come from the south of England, outside London, North Wales – all to see the old feller! I sat down on the nearest chair and two or three came up to me, and then a woman came up to me. I had never seen her before – she must have been getting on for seventy. She said, "Are you Mr Roberts?" "I am." "Did you know my grandfather?" "I don't know who your grandfather was." "It was Mr Shufflebottom." He was the headmaster before me. I said, "Yes, I just saw him for about an hour." In the November before I started in the January, I got a letter from Spurley Hey, the Director of Education. He wanted me to go across to St Luke's to have a word with the headmaster, see the teachers and get used to things. This I did, and it was the only time I ever saw him. She said, "I think you were marvellous." Then these people came up to me and spoke to me and I've never been kissed so much in my life! They were in their fifties, you know. They said, "You won't know me, you'll have forgotten." I said, "I haven't!"

A beautifully dressed lady came up to me by herself; I didn't like her to think I didn't know who she was, so I didn't ask her her name. She said, "Do you know, Mr Roberts, when I left school I bought some of the songs you taught us at this school, like Handel's 'Largo' and 'Who is Sylvia?' Almost every weekend I go into my lounge, sit down at the piano and sing those songs, and they do bring back happy memories of you." Wasn't that nice? I had a lovely time that night – I got there at six and didn't leave until half past nine. The fellows came up to me – "Have you still got it in your pocket, the strap?" I said, "No, I've not got it tonight!"

There was Peter Carter, whom I had taught and he had married a girl from the school. He was in his fifties, and I said, "Ee Peter, do you remember that day I came round to look at you while you were having the art lesson? You were in Standard 5. I got in front of you and saw a packet of cigarettes in your top pocket. So I took them out and said, 'Whose are these, Peter?' You said, 'They're mine, Mr Roberts.'" His mother and father must have died when he was young, his aunt was bringing him up – she had a milliner's shop on Hulme Hall Lane. I said, "Does your aunt know you smoke?" "No, sir." "Well, we'll have to tell your aunt about this." He wasn't a strong boy at all. So I put my hat on and went across

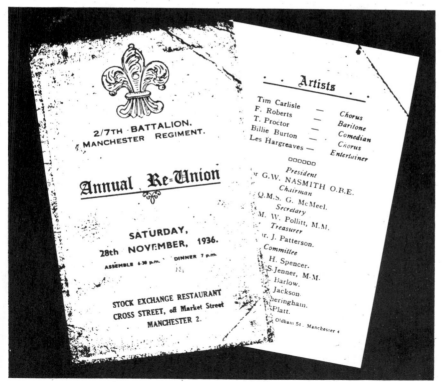

A card from a re-union dinner of the 2/7th Manchester Regiment, with Fred Roberts among the entertainers.

Teachers at St Luke's. Fred Roberts is standing in the centre

to see her. I said, "Look what I've found in Peter's pocket." She said, "Well, I don't know - he's been coming home from church on Sunday mornings looking as pale as a ghost, not wanting any dinner and feeling so sick." I said, "He and the other beggars have been having a smoke in the cemetery on the way home!" He remembered it!

I had another case of smoking. One of the men teachers came to my room one day with a packet of Woodbines, when there were five in a packet. The teacher said, "I've just found these in the yard." I said, "Oh, they'll be Tommy Millership's, the caretaker's. He's always walking about with a packet of Woodbines half out of his waistcoat pocket. I'll go across and see him; he lives not far from school." So I knocked on the door and Tommy came out. I said, "Are these yours, Tommy?" "No, I've got mine here, see." And there they were. So I went back to the top class of boys and said, "These have been found in the school yard." Well, you should have seen the lads' faces, they were every one guilty! "Do they belong to anybody? I wouldn't like to think they belonged to anybody, but do they?" All was quiet, and at last Jack Wogan put his hand up. "What do you know about them, Jack?" "Well, if there's one missing, Mr Roberts, it might be my packet." "There is one missing, Jack, so they must be yours." All was quiet again. "Do you expect to get them back again, Jack?" "No, sir." "Why not?" "Well, I know you don't smoke and you won't agree with me smoking." Well, I had to give them back as they were his property. He was a nice lad, Jack was. He was killed in the navy.

When the school leaving age was raised to fifteen I decided I would have to find something else for the boys to do. It wasn't as if St Luke's was a big council school with science labs and the like. So I decided to send a class of fifteen boys to cookery lessons. I saw the cookery mistress and told her what I wanted. She said, "What a good idea, but I'd be frightened of boys." I said, "They're all right, they're a nice lot of boys." So she went down to see the Director of Education at Deansgate, who thought it was a good idea. I sent fifteen boys every Tuesday morning to cookery, and they were delighted. Then, a fortnight before Christmas, they were all assembled on the Tuesday morning and I went to inspect them. Several of them had little bottles in their hands. One had brandy, another had gin, another had some wine. I said, "What's this about?" "Please sir, we're mixing the Christmas cake today, so Mother's sent this to put in the mixture." So they went and made their Christmas cakes. On the Tuesday before we broke up for Christmas they all came to my room door with the Christmas cakes they had made, beautiful, decorated cakes. They were as pleased as punch and I said, "Well, I am delighted. You have done well. Well, you're going to be luckier than Mrs Roberts and I, we haven't got the ingredients." (It was in the days of food rationing and you had to go and queue outside the provision shop for two and a half ounces of butter.) They went off and on the Friday morning just about ten minutes before we closed the school, a knock came on my door and it was a parent of one of these boys with a Christmas cake in her hand. I said, "What's this all about, Mrs Quick?" She said, "There's been no pleasure in our house since Tuesday. Our John's been walking about the house saying, 'Poor Mr and Mrs Roberts won't have a Christmas cake. Oh I am sorry for them!' I was forced to make this cake and bring it to you!" That was kind, wasn't it? I met one of those boys when I went to that reunion.

I remember one boy, Peter James, he was a nice little lad, but oh he had a terrible temper! The teacher would say something to me about what he had been doing and I'd go into the class to speak to Peter. He would start wriggling while I was talking to him and before I had finished I was talking to his back. When his time came for leaving school, I asked him what he wanted to do. "I would like to go and work on a farm, Mr Roberts." "I'll see what I can do for you." So on my way home I called at the YMCA and got talking to somebody. In a few weeks I got a call from them to say they had found Peter a job on a lovely farm in Derbyshire, but he'd have to live in. Of course, he wanted that and he did enjoy it. He used to come home on a fortnight's leave and he always came into school to see me. Then one afternoon one of the teachers was taking the top class for PT and he came up to me and said, "Peter James has been standing at the gate outside." I said, "Has he? It's funny he didn't come upstairs to see me." He said, "No, he walked away." An hour afterwards two detectives were in school. Peter had done an awful deed; he was tried and found guilty and was sent to Wakefield prison for life. But he was let out before his life imprisonment was up.

One day, after I had retired, the parson of St Paul's, Withington, telephoned me and said, "They're letting Peter James home from Wakefield to Strangeways for a month to talk to his parents and friends. Would you like to go? He'd be glad to see you." So we went to Strangeways. Oh what a sight! There was a big, long counter in this hall and all the relations were sitting on one side and the prisoners were on the other behind a wire affair. Griffin, the parson, and I stood there and then this fellow came up and said the Governor didn't want us to sit with those people, but to use his room. So we went to the Governor's little sitting room. Peter was brought in to us and we had a nice talk, but it was most difficult to talk to him. We didn't want to talk to him about prison life so we got him talking about some of his old school mates and what they were doing. Then the officer came in and said, "I'm afraid your time's up now, you'll have to go." So I stood up and said, "Well Peter, you've still got that lovely smile on your face that you had as a schoolboy. Keep that, lad and it'll help you through life." And he just sobbed, broke his heart and sobbed.

Then some time after that a knock came to our door and it was Peter. I suppose he'd be about 28 or 29. I was glad to see him and Jessie made him some tea. He had come out of prison and he was living with his father. I think we gave him some flowers, because he had been to see us once as a boy - walking to our house all the way from Miles Platting. We gave him a bunch of flowers then and he thought he was taking the Crown jewels home!

****

44

The following appreciation of Fred Roberts appeared in the parish magazine of St Luke's in 1948:

Mr Fred Roberts

"Good-bye, Mr Chips." So said the boys in the famous story as they bade farewell to a schoolmaster who was so much more than a schoolmaster.

Later this year the boys and girls of St Luke's Day Schools will say "Good-bye" to a real life "Mr Chips" when Mr Fred Roberts closes the door of his "Little room upstairs" for the last time after 50 years in the service of youth, 20 of which he has spent as Headmaster of St Luke's.

He has held a unique position in our Parish life during that period, for no man wields a greater influence over the future of our children than a schoolmaster. In Mr Roberts we have a man equally devoted to the causes of Education and Christianity, and who has continually advocated the closest possible co-operation between the Sunday School and the Day School, toward the better education and future welfare of the child.

Mr Roberts is a happy man when the scholars of his Day School take their places in the Church and sing their Christmas Carols under his baton, and the numbers present in the pews on those occasions bear fitting testimony to his zeal for this perfect Union. We were delighted when Mr Roberts told us that the Children's Carol Services were the outstanding memories of an eventful career.

And what of that career? Well, he was a pupil teacher at the age of 13 at St Mark's Day School, Holland Street, for which he was paid exactly 2/1d per week. After service in the first World War he taught at Brookdale Park and Holland Street Municipal Schools. He came to St Luke's Church as Choirmaster in 1922 and six years later he became ours altogether when he was appointed head of St Luke's Day School (Boys Department). The three departments were amalgamated in 1933 and Mr Roberts was appointed School Headmaster.

He is a man of many interests. A lover of all sports, he recalls with pride his playing days with North East Manchester Cricket Club, on whose ground the present Newton Heath "Avro" factory now stands. He is an enthusiastic gardener and believes that all teachers should be gardeners because of the wealth of knowledge to be acquired in this hobby. He is a delightful raconteur of schoolboy stories, as a speaker he is amongst the most popular visitors to the Men's Class and his love of Choral Music is well known to all of us at St Luke's.

A lifetime with children has left him still a young man at heart and it is typical of his outlook that he speaks in praise of the newcomers to the profession - the Government-trained ex-Servicemen.

Mr Roberts loves the children of Miles Platting and will miss their company and their laughter, their confidences and their problems, and he is deeply appreciative of the sublime trust with which they place themselves in his care. Yes, he will miss his children and they will miss him too, but his retirement will not be lonely with the possession of so many memories.

Mr Roberts paid a tribute, during our chat, to the parents of St Luke's children. He said they had always been his friends and had seldom found them unresponsive when he had cause to approach them for help with his work amongst their children.

Mr Fred Roberts is certainly a St Luke's personality - a valued member of our community - and we in the Church are grateful to know that we shall still have his presence, his help and advice at our disposal even after he has said good-bye to the class rooms.

And the children will still be able to see their old friend again at least once a year on Shrove Tuesday evening. He is booked for years to come as Master of Ceremonies to the Mardi Gras. The lads will not consider any other applicant for the job.

In conclusion, a word about Mr Roberts' life-partner, herself a former St Mark's School teacher. We haven't the space to write very much about this charming lady, but we will say that she makes the tastiest lemon cheese we have tasted in years! Thank you again, Mrs Roberts.

Notes

When Fred Roberts was born, Manchester was very different from the city we know today. Areas such as Rusholme, Bradford, Harpurhey and Crumpsall had yet to be incorporated within its boundaries and the magnificent Town Hall was just seven years old. Horse trams were still a novelty, having only just been introduced, and Trafford Park was a vast expanse of green fields. The opening of the Manchester Ship Canal was still ten years away.

Manchester was the "Cottonopolis", a bustling Victorian workhouse extolling the virtues of private enterprise and the "Manchester School" of laissez-faire economics. Some of the cotton mills and engineering works described by Fred can still be seen in parts of Miles Platting and Ancoats. When he was young the canals of the area, the Rochdale in particular, were busy highways for the horse-drawn boats bringing raw materials for local industry and taking away the finished products.

The social life of the working class districts in Victorian Manchester was very limited. The twelve hour working day was quite common and children of twelve years of age were still allowed to work part time in the factories.

Housing left a lot to be desired - lodging houses, cellar dwellings, back-to-backs and shared outside lavatories were common. The water supply could be a tap in the yard or, at best, piped cold water; this was before the days of the fine Thirlemere water supply. Cooking was carried out on the coal fire or in the ovens alongside. Lighting was very often by paraffin lamps, with candles to take upstairs to bed if you could be trusted!

It is little wonder that many people sought warmth and comfort in the nearest pub. Once through its welcoming doors, they could escape reality with the aid of the brewers' opium. Others relied on spiritual guidance from the many churches, missions and ragged schools. Working class areas had many caring clergymen and priests fighting a mammoth battle against poverty and political apathy.

In 1878 the British army marched into Afghanistan and during 1880 and 1881 the (63rd) 1st Battalion Manchester Regiment had garrisoned the city of Kandahar. Just before the start of the twentieth century they were in action again at Elanslaagte, and later at the seige of Ladysmith. Privates J Pitts and R Scott won the Victoria Cross at Caesar's Camp on 7th January 1900. Fourteen years later it was the turn of the 2nd Battalion (96th), who formed part of Smith Dorrien's division at Le Cateau. After the stand of the 26th August 1914 the Battalion had lost 14 officers and 339 men. In the Great War this famous old regiment provided over forty battalions, probably equal to the size of the present British army. After the 1st and 2nd Battalions came the turn of the Territorial Army, and the first T.A. division to leave these shores was the local 42nd East Lancs, which included the Manchester Brigade decimated at Gallipoli in 1915. Next followed Kitchener's army and this city provided eight "Pals" battalions, including a bantam battalion. At the Battle of the Somme in 1916, ten battalions of the

Manchesters were committed. Mercifully, after this disastrous campaign the idea of men drawn from warehouses and workshops belonging to one city was never revived. Many of the survivors of this action were soon in action again in the notorious salient of Ypres, considered by many old soldiers as the worst posting on the Western Front.

Fred describes going to see Johnny Clynes at a local venue. Clynes was one of a small number of Labour Members of Parliament who entered the House of Commons in 1906. He was the member for East Manchester, which became the Platting Division. The son of an Irish labourer, Clynes was born in Oldham in 1868, and through the Union movement he joined the Labour Party. In 1923 he proposed the vote of no confidence which brought down Baldwin's Government and, supported by the Liberals, the first Labour Government took office. He became Lord Privy Seal and Deputy Leader; from 1929 until 1931 he was the Home Secretary.

Manchester's ratepayers received a great deal of revenue from public enterprises - gas, electricity, water, etc. Hydraulic power was very popular and Manchester had three pumping stations providing power for such things as lifts and packing presses. The sole remaining station stands on Water Street near to Albert Bridge. With the transfer of the public utilities to the nationalised sector the city has lost many valuable assets.

The health of the people has improved vastly in the twentieth century, but planners made many mistakes when they started to rehouse the population from the inner city areas like Miles Platting and Hulme. These people were the bedrock of the city; their common bond of warmth and friendship has been lost, perhaps for ever.

Frank Heaton

Working class children in Angel Meadow, on the occasion of the opening of an extension to Charter Street Ragged School in 1910